THE KIOWA

by Victoria Sherrow

Illustrated by Richard Smolinski

ROURKE PUBLICATIONS, INC.

VERO BEACH, FLORIDA 32964

CONTENTS

© 1997 by Rourke Publications, Inc.

Library of Congress Cataloging-in-Publication Data

Sherrow, Victoria.
    The Kiowa / by Victoria Sherrow; illustrated by Richard Smolinski.
        p. cm. — (Native American people)
    Includes index.
    Summary: Surveys various aspects of Kiowa culture, including family life and daily activities, hunting and food gathering, clothing, games, religion, and social organization.
    ISBN 0-86625-605-9
    1. Kiowa Indians—History—Juvenile literature. 2. Kiowa Indians—Social life and customs—Juvenile literature. [1. Kiowa Indians. 2. Indians of North America.]
    I. Smolinski, Dick, ill. II. Title. III. Series.
E99.K5S54 1997
973'.04975—dc21   97-7831
                                                 CIP
                                                  AC

Introduction

For many years, archaeologists—and other people who study early Native American cultures—believed that the first humans to live in the Americas arrived in Alaska from Siberia between 11,000 and 12,000 years ago. Stone spear points and other artifacts dating to that time were discovered in many parts of the Americas.

The first Americans probably arrived by way of a vast bridge of land between Siberia and Alaska. The land link emerged from the sea when Ice Age glaciers lowered the level of the world's oceans.

The first migration across the bridge was most likely an accident. It appears that bands of hunters from Asia followed herds of mammoths, giant bison, and other Ice Age game that roamed the 1,000-mile-wide bridge. Over a long time—perhaps thousands of years—some of the hunters arrived in Alaska.

Many scholars now suggest that the first Americans may have arrived in North America as early as 30,000 or even 50,000 years ago. Some of these early Americans may not have crossed the bridge to the New World. They may have arrived by boat, working their way down the west coasts of North America and South America.

In support of this theory, scientists who study language or genetics (the study of the inherited similarities and differences found in living things) believe that there may have been many migrations of peoples over the bridge to North America. There are about 200 different Native American languages, which vary greatly. In addition to speaking different languages, groups of Native Americans can look as physically different as, for example, Italians and Swedes. These facts lead some scientists to suspect that multiple migrations started in different parts of Asia. If this is true, then Native Americans descend not from one people, but from many.

After they arrived in Alaska, different groups of early Americans fanned out over North and South America. They inhabited almost every corner of these two continents, from the shores of the Arctic Ocean in the north to Tierra del Fuego, at the southern tip of South America. Over this immense area, there were many different environments, which changed with the passage of time. The lifestyles of early Americans adapted to these environments and changed with them.

In what is now Mexico, some Native Americans built great cities and developed agriculture. Farming spread north. So did the concentration of people in large communities, which was the result of successful farming. In other regions, agriculture was not as important. Wild animals and plants were the main sources of food for native hunters and gatherers, such as the thirty-one Native American tribes who lived in the Great Plains area of America.

One of these tribes was the Kiowa. Groups of Kiowa lived in the southern plains around present-day Colorado and northern Texas. A related group called the Kiowa Apache lived in what is now Oklahoma.

The Kiowa language is related to the Pueblo Tanoan language, which is linked to the Native American language group called "Uto-Aztecan." Kiowan was spoken in the region that occupies Oklahoma, Kansas, and Colorado.

Origins of the Kiowa

The name "Kiowa" comes from the word *kaigwa*, which means "principal people." According to legend, the Kiowa people came from the upper Yellowstone River Valley of central Montana. They claimed that in earlier times, their ancestors lived in the Black Hills of South Dakota, where the Kootenai were their neighbors. The Kiowa migrated south to the Great Plains sometime after 1742.

A nomadic people, the Kiowa moved about with the seasons. Before the horse reached the Great Plains during the 1700s, the Kiowa traveled on foot. The buffalo, also called bison, supplied most of their food and many other needs, as was true for other Native Americans living on the Plains. The Kiowa did not fish or farm, and did not gather many wild plants for food.

The tribe developed an advanced system of pictographic signs, or painted symbols, that came close to being a written language. These symbols, painted on animal hides, were used to record events and to keep calendars. By studying these pictures, historians have learned much about the history and traditions of the Kiowa.

Daily Life

The Kiowa were a relatively small tribe. By the 1700s, they numbered about 3,000. The tribe was divided into seven smaller groups called "bands." By living in groups, they could hunt more successfully and defend themselves against enemies.

The Kiowa worked hard to meet their basic needs on the dry and rugged Plains, especially for food. Most of the Great Plains received only about 20 inches of rainfall each year, and temperatures varied widely with the seasons. In addition, the Kiowa and other Plains tribes had to contend with blizzards, hailstorms, tornadoes, and strong, hot winds. The harsh climate made farming difficult, if not impossible.

The Kiowa did not stay in one village year-round. They traveled in order to find the best hunting grounds. In winter, they usually settled in villages.

To suit their nomadic lifestyle, the Kiowa lived in lightweight but sturdy shelters called *tipis*. They were made of strips of buffalo skin supported by wooden poles. A person's status in the tribe and the size of the family determined the size of the *tipi*. A flap of buffalo skin served as a door.

Tipis were moved from one encampment to another as the seasons changed. They were easily built, taken apart, and put back together. They could be made larger or smaller if a family's need for space changed.

Tipis contained simple furnishings. For example, beds usually consisted of buffalo robes arranged on the ground.

Clothing, eating utensils, tools, and weapons were among the other possessions that the Kiowa kept inside their *tipis*. A fire was built in the center of the *tipi* to provide warmth and heat for cooking. The smoke rose out through a hole in the top, where two ear-like flaps were moved around to change the direction of the smoke.

Groups of *tipis* were arranged in a circle. Families had their own dwellings, but visiting was common. A closed *tipi* flap was a sign that the occupants did not want any visitors.

The Kiowa lived in **tipis**, *which they took with them when they moved to new hunting grounds.*

The Kiowa relied greatly on the buffalo for their day-to-day needs. Hunting these animals and preparing the meat and skins took much of their time. From the buffalo came food, clothing, bedding, *tipi* coverings, and tools. The Kiowa dried and hardened the skin from the animal's neck to make circular shields. They wet strips of rawhide, or untanned skin from the buffalo, and then used these wet pieces to tie the tops of hammers and clubs to their handles. As the rawhide dried, it shrank, holding the two parts firmly together.

Family Life

The Kiowa lived in nuclear families consisting of a mother, father, and their children. Sometimes, grandparents lived with them as well. Families belonged to larger groups called clans, which were named after animals, such as the Elk or Bear. Members of a clan took a special interest in the welfare of fellow members, especially the children. Clan traditions were important in tribal ceremonies.

Marriages were sometimes arranged by the parents of the young couple. People were not allowed to marry those to whom they were related by blood. Most men had only one wife, but it was permissible to have more than one if a man could support them. A man sometimes married one of his wife's sisters.

Infants were carried around strapped securely on wooden cradle boards, which were covered with animal skins. A baby moved about during the day with the mother, and was fed and cared for when necessary. From their cradle boards, Kiowa babies could watch people working and playing and see the changing scenes of nature.

On the Plains, children learned from their earliest days to be rugged and able to fend for themselves. When a male child was born, he was plunged into cold water, even in the wintertime. As a future warrior, he had to become strong for the demanding life ahead.

Girls were also raised to be physically strong. Both boys and girls learned to use weapons. They were praised for showing courage and for winning games of skill and strength.

Children learned to ride and to care for horses at an early age. As they grew older, young people received larger and faster horses. Boys looked forward to the day they would join the men on a buffalo hunt. In the meantime, they and their sisters were expected to do chores, such as fetching water and gathering wood for fires. Older girls helped to prepare food and to care for younger children.

The Kiowa worked for the community, as well as for themselves, to help the tribe survive. Younger hunters shared buffalo or other game they caught with those who did not have enough to eat—for example, the elderly, the sick, or widows.

While strapped to their cradle boards, babies could watch their mothers work or rest comfortably.

There was a clear division of jobs among different members of the tribe. Men were hunters, warriors, chiefs, and spiritual leaders. They made tools and weapons. Women cared for the homes and children, and they prepared and stored food.

A man records an important event by painting symbols on an animal hide.

A Kiowa woman boils dried strips of buffalo meat.

10

Kiowa women also made and decorated the family's clothing and other household objects. They painted the skins of their *tipis* and their buffalo robes with elaborate designs, such as pictures of buffalo.

Rawhide was a versatile material. The Kiowa used it to make saddle covers for women, bags for their cooking tools, and the soles of moccasins. Women also enjoyed decorating the rawhide bags known as "parfleches," which were used to store food and carry things during a trip. These pouch-like bags were made of whole hides and had three rounded sides. After clothing, food, or other objects were placed in the parfleche, the sides were drawn up and folded, then laced tightly with strips of rawhide.

The designs women painted on household items included events from their daily lives, such as important battles or adventures they had. Black and white bands symbolized the night and the stars. The color red stood for earth, as well as for blood and sunset. On their own clothing and belongings, women liked to paint triangular and diamond-shaped patterns.

Food

Like other tribes living on the dry Plains, the Kiowa did not raise crops. There were also not many wild foods that could be gathered because only some of the berries, seeds, and roots that grew on the land were edible. Meat, mostly from buffalo, was the tribe's main food. They made good use of the various parts of the buffalo, which was so vital to their survival. People of all ages ate buffalo meat.

Even children who did not yet have any teeth were given chunks to suck on. In the summertime, when buffalo were most plentiful in the region, the Kiowa ate the choicest parts of the animal. The tongue was regarded as a treat. Each year, the first buffalo meal of spring was eagerly enjoyed. All of the edible parts of the animal were consumed during the lean days of winter, when buffalo and other game were scarce.

Antelope, deer, and elk were the other game meats eaten by the Kiowa. Sometimes, they found birds' eggs to make a meal. Through trade with other tribes, the Kiowa occasionally acquired small quantities of corn, beans, or squash. The Plains tribes that raised crops, such as the Osage, rarely had enough for their own needs, however, much less any food to spare.

When fresh meat was not available, the Kiowa ate preserved meat. A common way to preserve meat for later use was to dry long, thin strips in the sun, then pack them between layers of berries and uncooked buffalo fat. Meat was also stored in the form of pemmican. To make pemmican, women used stone hammers to pound dried meat into pulp. They mixed this pulp with buffalo fat and set it aside in parfleches.

Hunting and Fishing

There were numerous animals on the Great Plains that the Kiowa could hunt. Larger game included buffalo, deer, antelope, sheep, mountain goats, and bears. Among the smaller prey were prairie dogs and foxes. A Kiowa boy was not allowed to join buffalo hunts until he was about thirteen

A group of men circle a herd of buffalo during a hunt. Their horses have been trained to come up along the right sides of the buffalo.

years old. Young boys practiced their hunting skills and found food for their villages by hunting rabbits, squirrels, and other small prey.

Before horses arrived on the Great Plains and made hunting easier, the Kiowa were known for their successful ways of hunting antelope. Groups of hunters chased herds of antelope into a confined section of the Little Missouri River Valley, where it was easier to kill the animals before they had a chance to escape. The Cheyenne and Arapaho learned this way of hunting from the Kiowa.

The Kiowa had clever methods for killing buffalo as well. Groups of hunters encircled a herd of buffalo, which confused the trapped animals, known for their poor eyesight. Some were shot with bows and arrows or spears as they tried to get away.

Once the Kiowa had horses, hunters caught far more buffalo. Before the late 1800s, buffalo were plentiful. At times, herds of these shaggy, black-furred animals seemed to cover the earth. Millions of them roamed the Plains. The Kiowa eagerly awaited the annual migration of the buffalo herds, which began after the worst winter weather had passed. Kiowa scouts set up *tipis* in areas where the herds usually passed. After locating the herds, the scouts notified the tribe. It was a time of singing, dancing, and rejoicing. A campsite was established near the place where the herd would run.

Riding alongside the herd of running buffalo, the hunter aimed at one animal, then another. The Kiowa's horses were trained to ride along the right sides of the moving buffalo, without coming too close. The Kiowa hunter aimed an arrow toward the animal's heart, launching a second one to cause quick death. While the older, more experienced hunters went after large buffalo, the boys followed on smaller horses, shooting any slow-moving animals they could find.

Killing a buffalo involved a certain amount of danger. A careless or un-skilled hunter might be knocked over and trampled by these enormous animals. A horse could trip, hurling its rider into the path of running buffalo.

After men killed the buffalo, women and girls skinned the animals and cut up the carcasses, which were then loaded onto horses. One buffalo might provide about 500 pounds of meat.

When a young man returned from his first successful hunt, other Kiowa offered him much praise. In his honor, the boy's family sometimes held a feast and gave gifts to needy villagers. A successful hunt was also a time when the Kiowa gave thanks to the spirits for the great gift of the buffalo. One often-recited prayer asked that the buffalo always be plentiful.

Clothing

From birth to death, the Kiowa used a variety of animal skins to clothe themselves and for blankets and bedding. Infants were wrapped in soft skins, which also covered their cradle boards.

Everyday clothing was simple and spare. In warm weather, Kiowa men often wore only breechcloths—lengths of animal skin that were wrapped around their hips. When they were in rough terrain they also wore leggings. Women wore loose, simple dresses and plain leggings.

A man and woman are dressed in summer clothing. Their animal-skin leggings protect their legs from scratches in rough terrain.

The Kiowa's main source of food, the buffalo, also provided them with much of their clothing. Strong and waterproof, buffalo hides made sturdy, long-lasting garments. The hides of the buffalo that hunters killed during the winter had very thick fur and made excellent robes, caps, blankets, mittens, and footwear. Thinner hides were used to make dresses, shirts, and leggings. The thinnest and softest hides, which came from young buffalo, were used for undergarments.

The Kiowa wore simple moccasins made from pieces of soft leather that were folded over and sewn to fit the owner's feet. Cold-weather moccasins were made from buffalo skins. The fur was worn on the inside, next to the foot. Ceremonial moccasins had brightly colored designs.

Ceremonial dress was much fancier than everyday clothing. Men donned war bonnets covered with large, bright feathers. Kiowa women wore dresses decorated with elk's teeth, which were worked into intricate patterns. It was not permissible for a woman to use more than two teeth from the same elk when decorating a garment. An elk's tooth dress therefore took a woman a long time to finish. A dress adorned with hundreds of elk's teeth showed that the owner's husband was an expert hunter.

In the absence of elk's teeth, women sewed porcupine quills or beads on their dresses. They also used imitation elk's teeth, carved from pieces of bone. After white people came to their region, the Kiowa traded goods for beads of various colors and shapes and added these to their clothing.

When they went into battle, men wore shirts with designs that were thought to protect them and bring success. Designs were painted on the shirts with dyes made from roots and berries or else sewn on with beads and porcupine quills.

Travel

Before the Kiowa acquired horses in the mid-1700s, they traveled about on foot and, occasionally, by canoe. The rivers in their region were not always navigable, so water travel was not a dependable way to get around.

Like many other Plains Indians, the Kiowa used the *travois* to carry their belongings when they traveled. This carrying device was made up of two poles and crossbars that formed a

shape like the letter "A." Dogs, the Kiowa's only domestic animal prior to the horse, pulled the *travois*. The pointed end was attached to the dog's back. A strong dog could carry a load weighing forty pounds a distance of about 5 or 6 miles in a day.

A dog pulls a travois, *which is loaded with the belongings of this woman's family.*

The Kiowa used sign language to communicate with other tribes. A man uses the signs for a white man (left) and a buffalo (right).

The Kiowa traded with Pueblo tribes living in present-day New Mexico and other regions of the Southwest. Words from the Pueblo languages became part of the Kiowa's vocabulary. Before 1750, the Kiowa lived in the Black Hills region, in present-day South Dakota. They also traded with the Arikari, who lived on the Missouri River. Later, they exchanged horses and articles they had obtained from the Spaniards for corn, tobacco, and vegetables raised in Arikari villages. Members of the Sarsi tribe often visited Kiowa villages during the 1700s, and their people intermarried. When trading with other tribes, Native Americans in the Plains used sign language.

The Kiowa were among the first Plains tribes to use horses in the 1730s. Tribes acquired horses through trade, by capturing those they found roaming on the range, or by stealing them.

The use of horses for transportation greatly changed life on the Plains. A horse-drawn travois could carry much heavier loads than one pulled by dogs—as much as 200 pounds. Horses could also travel twice as far as dogs in a day. On horseback, the Kiowa could follow the buffalo herds, which ensured that the Kiowa would not starve. For these reasons, horses were a measure of a family's wealth, and they were highly valued as gifts.

Games

For Kiowa children, play was often connected with the kind of work they would do as adults. For instance, Kiowa boys fought make-believe battles in preparation for the time when they would be young warriors. They also pretended to hunt buffalo and had shooting matches using bows and arrows. Girls played house with dolls and child-sized *tipis*. They learned to put up and take down their small buffalo-skin *tipis*, just as their mothers did with real *tipis*. They learned to sew by making clothing for their dolls.

Much childhood fun took place outdoors. Children enjoyed games and had dogs and other pets, including raccoons or birds they tamed themselves. During the winter, children slid along the Great Plains' ice-covered rivers on sleds with runners made from buffalo bones. Throughout the year, they played games while riding on horseback.

Toys were simple. They were made from materials found in the Kiowa's natural environment. Babies played with carved bones, hooves, and other objects attached to the side of the cradle board. Older children tossed pine cones, aiming for the inside of a circle made from a tree limb.

Adults enjoyed leisure activities, too. Contests of skill in shooting bows and arrows, running, and horseback riding were popular. One game the Kiowa enjoyed in summer was played with a small ball made of animal hair. Each player used a curved stick made from cherry wood to hit this ball to one of the other players.

Another outdoor game involved rolling a hoop along the ground with a pole. A form of lacrosse was played on ice during the winter months. Two teams of players used sticks with nets on one end to move a ball toward the goal. The Kiowa also played guessing games, some of which involved gambling. Dice games were played with marked plum pits.

Kiowa children built child-size tipis for fun and also to learn skills they would use later in life as adults.

20

Political and Social Organization

Kiowa leaders were men chosen on the basis of their courage, wisdom, and ability to lead the people. Kiowa chiefs did not inherit their positions. Nor did they have complete control over their people. One of their main roles was to settle arguments among members of the tribe. A tribal council of male leaders made important decisions. Others were allowed to express their opinions.

The laws that governed the Kiowa's behavior were intended to protect the whole group. Murder was forbidden, as was the destruction of another person's property or the taking of his or her horse. A person who committed a serious crime might be driven out of the tribe or forced to give up all of his or her property.

Strict rules governed the buffalo hunt. All Kiowa hunters were supposed to wait for the hunt to begin. If anyone disturbed the buffalo herd or started hunting on his own, he was dishonored and his weapons were destroyed. The chief appointed trustworthy people to make sure that everyone obeyed the rules of the hunt.

The Kiowa were among the fiercest warriors on the Plains and were known for launching attacks on other tribes. With their powerful and effective military organization, Kiowa fighters were feared by their enemies.

Most Kiowa men grew up to be warriors as well as hunters. As children, they were taught how to shoot small arrows, graduating to larger and sharper ones as they grew older. Through practice, they learned to hit moving targets.

Young men became warriors during their late teens. To signal their new positions, they made strong shields from buffalo skin. They learned to make bows and arrows and hatchets, which were the most common weapons before white men brought guns and ammunition into the region. Within the tribe, male fighters became members of warrior societies, where

This young man is dressed in the ceremonial clothing and war paint that Kiowa men wore when going into battle.

A man makes an arrow that will be used by a hunter or warrior. On the right is a shield made from buffalo hide.

they were ranked according to their exploits and courage in battle. Killing an enemy earned them high praise.

The Kiowa were allied with the Apache and Comanche, also known as expert horsemen and warriors. Among the enemies of the Kiowa were the Sioux, who lived to the north. At one time, the Cheyenne were the Kiowa's enemies, but later the Kiowa joined them to fight against white soldiers.

Religious ceremonies were important in a tribe's preparation for war. The Kiowa believed that close ties to the supernatural world would protect them in battle. They tried to have dreams and visions of strong, fierce animal spirits that would help them defeat their enemies.

By the age of forty, Kiowa men were no longer expected to take part in war activities. At that age, they were eligible to join the tribal council and become political leaders.

Religious Life

The Kiowa's religion was part of their daily lives as well as major life events. The Kiowa thought that maintaining close ties with the spirit world would bring success in hunting, fighting, and healing. They called upon these friendly spirits in times of need.

In order to summon these spirits, the Kiowa men went on vision quests. A young man first went on a vision quest during his teens. He fasted (went without food) and went off alone to a quiet place. Eventually, he had a vision, or dream. The main figure in the dream, usually an animal, represented the young man's spirit helper for life.

Shamans—spiritual leaders and healers—led important religious rites and were called upon to help the sick. They sang special healing chants, and they knew the uses of various rituals and charms. The shamans took great care of the Kiowa medicine bundles that were used to protect the tribe. They were brought out only at special times.

Since buffalo were vital to the tribe's survival, the Kiowa held religious ceremonies before and after a hunt. When buffalo were scarce, ceremonies might be held to bring the hunters better luck in finding game.

Like many Plains groups, the Kiowa held a summer ceremony called the Sun Dance. It was an important occasion for the tribe, and all adults were required to attend. Members of the Kiowa-Apache band often joined the Kiowa for this Sun Dance. The ceremony was performed around the time of the annual buffalo hunt, when the tribe came together for a week and formed a large, circular encampment. During the week, short ceremonies took place. It was a time for praying and making special requests to the gods.

Just before the Sun Dance began, a *tipi* was pitched in the center of the camp. Secret rites were carried out there by the priests and select members of the tribe.

The chief performer and leader of the Kiowa Sun Dance, called a *kodu*, was the shaman. He carried a 2-foot-tall medicine doll that resembled a human figure. The doll wore a robe of white feathers and had symbols painted all over its body.

The Sun Dance lasted for four days, during which men performed special dances and people fasted. The main

performer, called a "keeper," danced on all four days. He was painted yellow to represent the sun and carried an eagle-bone whistle and a bunch of cedar branches. When the ceremonies were over, people joined together in the dance lodge to celebrate.

When someone died, the Kiowa buried him or her and recited special songs and prayers of mourning. When a warrior died, he was buried along with his horse. The Kiowa believed that the horse and its rider should be together in the afterlife.

When a Kiowa man went on a vision quest, he fasted until he had a vision or dream. The main animal or person in the dream was his spirit helper.

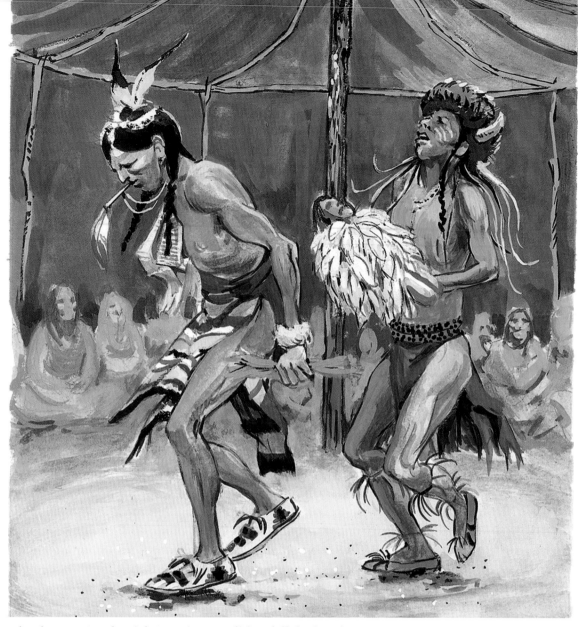

The shaman (on the right) carries a medicine doll during the Sun Dance.

European Contact

The Spanish explorer Francisco Vasquez de Coronado and his army crossed the Great Plains in 1541. They were mounted on horses—animals the Plains tribes had never seen. These 200 Spaniards carried lances and wore metal armor and helmets, which must have startled the Native Americans. With them were foot soldiers and hundreds of extra horses, cattle, sheep, and pack mules. On their trip across the Great Plains, Coronado and his soldiers encountered the nomadic Apache tribe.

Half a century after Coronado's visit, Spaniards established settlements in what is now the American Southwest. The Native Americans in the Southwest were able to obtain and raise horses and other livestock the Spaniards introduced into the region. The horse made its way north, and by the 1740s, nearly every tribe in the Great Plains had horses.

In addition to the Spaniards, other white men were coming to the Plains as well. French fur trappers sought the skins of deer, antelope, and other animals that were then in great demand in Europe. Besides catching animals themselves, they traded with the Native Americans for more of these furs and for buffalo robes. In exchange for their fur pelts and robes, the Kiowa and other Plains tribes obtained metal tools, cooking pans and utensils, guns, ammunition, and iron, which they could make into arrowheads.

In addition to these goods, foreigners brought new diseases with them, such as smallpox and measles, to which the Native Americans had no natural resistance. The foreigners also aggravated conflicts between different groups of Native Americans, who competed over trade with whites. Now that they were armed and on horseback, the tribes fought more deadly battles to gain territory and trading advantages.

Except for Spanish and French traders, the Kiowa did not encounter many whites during the 1700s. The tribe continued to hunt buffalo and follow their traditions. During the 1790s, they were living in villages near the Cheyenne and Arapaho along the upper Cheyenne River. The Kiowa remained on friendly terms with these tribes.

The world of the Plains tribes changed greatly during the next century. In 1781, after fighting the Revolutionary War, the American colonists won their independence from England and formed a new nation, the United States. More European settlers came to North America. The fur trade flourished as adventurous trappers from the eastern states, called "mountain men," came west.

In 1803, the United States purchased the Louisiana Territory—lands between the Mississippi River and the Rocky Mountains—from France. President Thomas Jefferson sent two men, Meriwether Lewis and William Clark, to explore this region.

In 1830, the U.S. government insisted that Native Americans who lived east of the Mississippi River give up their lands to white settlers and move west. The long, sad journey that these Native Americans made on foot is called the Trail of Tears. The eastern tribes moved chiefly to Oklahoma, where many of the Plains tribes lived. The U.S. government called the region Indian Territory. Armed U.S. soldiers patrolled the region. The government sent the tribes cooking utensils, beef, clothing, knives, and other items, but the supplies often did not arrive.

In addition to the newcomer tribes, white settlers passed through the Plains in covered wagons on their way to rich farmland in Oregon and California. By the 1850s, gold was discovered in California, and more people surged westward. White missionaries came to live among Native Americans to convert them to Christianity, although many tribes did not wish to be converted. The U.S. Congress encouraged western settlement by naming states and territories all the way to the Pacific Ocean.

As easterners passed through Kiowa hunting grounds, they disturbed the buffalo herds and their grazing lands. The Kiowa and other tribes attacked the settlers, hoping to discourage whites from coming onto their lands.

From 1855 to 1895, fighting between the Kiowa and U.S. troops and white

settlers continued. In a treaty signed in 1865, the Kiowa were assigned to live on a piece of land that included a section of western Texas, but whites living there would not give up that land. The Kiowa also disliked the government's plan to give them rations of food and goods in exchange for their hunting grounds. They preferred their former way of life.

No tribe resisted giving up its land longer or more persistently than the Kiowa. In 1868, however, the Kiowa were defeated by U.S. troops led by Lieutenant Colonel George Armstrong Custer. The Kiowa were forced onto a reservation in the Oklahoma Territory.

A Kiowa leader named Satanta led a group of warriors out of the confinement of the reservation. Together with a group of Comanche, the Kiowa engaged in guerrilla warfare in five states for several years.

In 1875, the Kiowa surrendered to U.S. officials at Fort Sill in Oklahoma. Again, they were taken to the reservation, where the Kiowa numbered about 1,070. War, smallpox, and cholera had killed hundreds of their people. In 1877, a measles epidemic killed hundreds more. By 1879, the buffalo, once the staple of the Kiowa diet, were almost gone from the Plains.

The Kiowa Today

After Oklahoma became a state in 1907, more Kiowa land was sold to whites. The Kiowa tried to learn new ways to survive and make a living. They received food and other goods from the government, but these were less than the government had promised them. Schools, such as the Chilocco

Indian Industrial School, were set up during the late 1800s. By 1919 about 170 students, including Kiowa, Comanche, Wichita, Cheyenne, and Arapaho, were enrolled at Chilocco. The government wanted Native Americans to give up their own cultures and adopt white ways and the Christian religion.

Toward that end, Congress passed the General Allotment Act (also called the Dawes Act) in 1887. This act broke up tribal reservation land into small

This woman's ceremonial dress is decorated with mollusk shells and brightly colored beads.

epidemic of 1877 and the disappearance of the buffalo in 1879. Kiowa George Poolaw kept the calendar going from 1893 until he died in 1939.

By the 1930s, the U.S. government was changing its policies and showing more respect for native cultures. During the Civil Rights Movement that swept across America during the 1950s and 1960s, Native Americans and other minorities who had been treated unfairly insisted on their rights and took new pride in their heritage. The Kiowa took a renewed interest in traditional songs, dances, crafts, and spiritual customs. That interest continues today.

According to the 1990 U.S. Census, there are 4,000 members of the Kiowa tribe in Oklahoma. The Sun Dance has been revived among the Kiowa and other tribes. Another positive change was the passage, in 1975, of the Indian Self-Determination Act. It allowed the Kiowa more opportunities to govern themselves.

Some well-known Kiowa have shared their heritage through literature and the arts. The author N. Scott Momaday won the Pulitzer Prize in 1969 for his novel *House Made of Dawn*. Another of his books, *The Way to Rainy Mountain*, was based on the history of the Kiowa.

During the 1920s, several artists known as the Kiowa Five worked at the University of Oklahoma. Their artwork was admired and sold around the country, as well as in France and Czechoslovakia. Some of their paintings depicted events from Kiowa history and ceremonies. Works by Kiowa artists can be seen at the Southern Plains Indian Museum and Craft Center in Anadarko.

Vanessa Paukeigope Morgan makes ceremonial Kiowa clothing in Anadarko, Oklahoma.

parcels, which were given to individual Native Americans. The millions of acres of reservation land that were left over were sold.

The Kiowa tried to preserve their culture. They continued to keep their pictograph calendars. The pictures, painted twice a year on buffalo skins, showed such events as the measles

Chronology

1541   Spanish explorer Francisco Vasquez de Coronado and his army cross the Great Plains and encounter Plains tribes.

1740s   The Kiowa obtain horses, as do other Plains tribes.

1803   The United States agrees to the Louisiana Purchase and buys from France lands between the Mississippi River and the Rocky Mountains.

1830   Many eastern Native American tribes move to the Plains during the Trail of Tears.

1850s   Many easterners pass through Kiowa hunting grounds as they head west.

1855   Fighting erupts between the Kiowa and U.S. soldiers and settlers; conflicts continue for forty years.

1865   The U.S. government gives the Kiowa a reservation that includes part of western Texas; settlers there refuse to leave.

1868   The Kiowa are defeated by U.S. troops and forced onto a reservation located in the Oklahoma Territory.

1875   The Kiowa surrender to U.S. officials at Fort Sill, Oklahoma.

1877   A measles epidemic kills hundreds of Kiowa.

1879   The buffalo are virtually gone from Kiowa hunting grounds.

1887   Congress passes the General Allotment Act (Dawes Act), which results in the loss of more land for the Kiowa and other tribes.

1975   After Congress passes the Indian Self-Determination Act, the Kiowa in Anadarko, Oklahoma, develop their own tribal government, based in Carnegie, Oklahoma.

INDEX

Acknowledgments and Photo Credits
Cover and all artwork by Richard Smolinksi.
Photographs on pages 8, 21, 29, and 30: David A. Harvey/©National Geographic Society.
Map by Blackbirch Graphics, Inc.

943